Bermuda Abstracts

MATRIX

Bermuda in 1630 by Guiljelmus Blaeu.

Mappa ÆSTIVARVM Insularum,
alias BARMVDAS dictarum, ad Ostia
Mexicani æstuarij jacentium in latitudine Gra:
duum 32 Minutorum 25 Ab Anglia, Londino
Scilicet versus Libonotum 3300 Miliaribus
Anglicanis, et a Roanoack (qui locus est
in Virginia) versus Euronotum 500 Mill.
accurate descripta.
Circa solstitium æstivum Anno 1616 solvere ex his Insulis
quinque viri, in Schapha superne aperta, trium doliorum
majorum capacitatis, et post septem hebdomadarum
navigationem omnes incolumes in Hiberniam appulerunt,
quale ab hominum memoria vix accidisse creditur
Scala trium Miliarum vel vigintiquatuor Stadiorum.
Amstelodami, Guiljelm Blaeuw excudit.
Plymouth
NOVA
New
England
HIBERNIA
ATVM
Burnt point
Prom ad ustum
S. GEORGES
ILAND
St. Davids
Iland.
Hammilton
Haring
toni Fretum
Harington
Sound
SOVTHAMTONIÆ PORTVS
Southampton Harbour
Pembroke
Tribe
Devonshire
Tribe
Smiths Tribe
Tribe
Part of
the Generall land
Warwick
Tribe
Pagets
Tribe
Pagets port
Gurnets head Hyrcæ promont.

Pisces © 1981

Designer: Cela Wright
Photographs edited by Cela Wright
Published in the United States of America by
Matrix Publications, Inc., Providence, Rhode Island

International Standard Book Number
Clothbound 0-936554-08-8
Paperbound 0-936554-09-6
Limited edition 0-936554-11-8
First edition 1982

Printed in the United States of America
by National Bickford Foremost

Bermuda Abstracts is distributed exclusively
in the United States by Matrix Publications,
Providence, Rhode Island

Bermuda: Paperback Distributors Co., Hamilton, Bermuda
Canada: Book Center, Montreal, Quebec
Great Britain: Argus Ltd., Watford, England
Italy: Idea Editions, Milan, Italy
Australia: Lamella, Sydney, Australia
All other world markets: Harper & Row,
Lindelaan, The Netherlands

Limited edition distributed exclusively by the
Windjammer Gallery
Reid & King Streets
Hamilton, Bermuda

Preceding photographs in order of appearance:

Blacksmith's Alley, St. George's
Angel's Delight, Smith's

Bermuda Abstracts

Photographs by Graeme Outerbridge

Preface by Landt Dennis

A Matrix Publication   Providence, Rhode Island

Preface

Photography records. Photographers see. Graeme Outerbridge, an internationally known Bermudian photographer, not only records and sees but interprets as well.

Bermuda is famous for its picture-postcard beauty—a blend of peaches and cream, clipped privet hedges, and sparkling beaches—and is easily captured on film, too easily, in fact. Outerbridge doesn't settle for facile effects. Like a scientist with a microscope, he looks for causes. Focusing on the island's historic houses and monuments, Outerbridge wants it understood that in photography, like mathematics, the whole is equal to its parts.

Outerbridge outlines the island's anatomy with his camera: chimneys, doors, and church steeples are bathed in sunlight; silhouetted against cobalt sky; dappled and divided by shadows. The results are hard-edged, two-dimensional abstracts—geometric juxtapositions of snow-blinding white and dazzling, sherbet-toned colors for which Bermuda is famous: pistachio green, blackberry mauve, carob beige, papaya yellow, mango orange. From a distance, Outerbridge's imagery is curious; close up, it is concise. Realizing that many people already know what Bermuda looks like, he shows us how he interprets his island home, leaving descriptive, pretty picture-postcard photography to the visitors and advertising agencies.

In the nineteenth and early twentieth centuries, photographers like Felice Beato, Francis Frith, and Georgis Sommers traveled the world, making a visual record of distant lands in order to provide photographs of those places most people would never see. Few people who traveled had the early, large-format cameras; those who did used them to supply the demand for photographs of the Jungfrau, the Coliseum, and the Eiffel Tower. The travel photography of today was known then as topographic photography, and

travel albums became both fashionable and fun.

James B. Heyl was one of Bermuda's camera pioneers at the end of the nineteenth century. He was so much an object of curiosity that the governor general of Bermuda, Major General J. H. Lefroy, and his entourage spent a day in 1875 watching Heyl work. Bermuda was known as the "Enchanted Isle" to early English sailors and was quick to catch the eye of the turn-of-the-century photographers, just as the island's mid-Atlantic location and fertile fields captured the attention of the British crown 200 years earlier.

Discovered but unclaimed by Spanish explorer Juan de Bermudez in 1503, Bermuda is a close gathering of four main islands and 116 islets, roughly 20 square miles in size. Bermuda is the fifth most densely populated nation in the world, with 55,000 local inhabitants. It is located over 840 miles from the nearest Bahamas and 640 miles from Cape Hatteras. Treacherous reefs lurk beneath the surface of Bermuda's turquoise sea, and early English mariners described it as the "Isles of the Devils." It is believed that Shakespeare had Bermuda in mind when he wrote *The Tempest.*

In 1609, Admiral Sir George Somers, commander of the *Sea Venture,* and his men were shipwrecked on Bermuda while carrying supplies to Jamestown. However, no lives were lost, and the 150 passengers stepped ashore onto a land outlined in pink coral sand, where temperatures rarely dipped below sixty degrees or rose above eighty degrees.

Discovering that "the devils that haunt the woods were but herds of swine," and that "the Fairies of the Rockes were but flockes of birds," Somers's crew spread the good news on their safe return to England.

The first official settlers arrived on the island in 1612, the year St. George's Town was founded. In 1620, now the oldest self-governing colony in the British Commonwealth, Bermuda began its parliament, making it the second oldest in the world after Virginia. Slaves were brought to the island, and in addition to working on plantations, they became servants, carpenters, and artisans.

Wealthy landowners—many of whom made fortunes in the trade between the Colonies, the West Indies, and Europe—built large houses from native limestone and stucco, with thick walls, massive outdoor chimneys, and supporting buttresses. These great houses with traces of medieval and Elizabethan design are so utilitarian and indigenous that they look as if they've grown out of the ground. They were made to withstand hurricanes and age.

Bermuda's architecture is unique and beautiful: an island heritage which is a delight to visitors and a rich harvest of impact-making images for Graeme Outerbridge. The scores of architectural landmarks, many of which have been superbly restored by private owners and the Bermuda Historic Society, are known for their "Welcoming Arms" staircases; butteries, or cold-storage houses, with pyramid roofs; scalloped, bowed, stepped, and classic gable ends; jalousie and eyebrow windows.

The building roofs are equally characteristic of Bermuda. Described by author and frequent visitor Mark Twain as "exactly like the white icing of a cake," they too are made out of native limestone, with overlapping slates that are traditionally covered with white lime wash. Used for catching rain, the roofs have helped solve the island's water problems for three centuries. In the last century Bermuda has become a destination attracting over 500,000 visitors a year.

After the Civil War, when shipbuilding and trade with America ceased to be profitable, Bermudians floundered in finding new

ways to earn a living. Princess Louise, Duchess of Argyll, the fourth daughter of Queen Victoria, and wife of the governor general of Canada saved the day when she decided to winter in Bermuda. Her arrival in 1883 was reported by the *New York Times*: "Queen's weather prevailed... doors and windows are open, flowers are blooming, people are wearing straw hats, and drinking sherry cobblers." The visit gave the island a name, triggered a stampede of rich Americans who wanted to follow in titled footsteps, and launched a tourist boom which hasn't stopped yet.

In the seventeenth century, The Reverend Michael Wigglesworth from Massachusetts became the first New World visitor to vacation in Bermuda. Fraught with illness and expecting to meet his maker on Bermuda, Wigglesworth quickly revived and turned a finale into an overture. He returned home, married twice more, sired innumerable additional offspring, and tended his flock for forty more years.

Steamship service to Hamilton from New York City for the last 100 years has included such superliners as the *S.S. Bermudian, Monarch of Bermuda, Queen of Bermuda,* and the *Ocean Monarch.* Free-spending Americans in the 1920s disembarked to check into such classic resorts as the Princess, Castle Harbour, Bermudiana, and the Mid-Ocean Club, all of which continue to be magnets for today's vacationers. In addition, there are more than 100 other resorts.

Golf and tennis, which were introduced into the United States from Bermuda by Mary Outerbridge, a distant relative of the photographer, have long been major island sports. Additional recreation includes stretching out on Bermuda's many beaches; shopping for Irish linen, English woolens, and French perfume at the numerous stores on Front Street; meandering on motorbikes along miles

of country roads bordered by lush, semitropical vegetation; and watching the cricket matches.

Reminders of Bermuda's British heritage and the island's courageous demand for civility in an era of turmoil linger gracefully on: the Bermuda Regiment and Cadets Pipe Band's performance of the age-old military ceremony of Beating Retreat; the annual Peppercorn Ceremony in St. George's; afternoon tea complete with scones and strawberry jam.

In the seventeenth century, Thomas Middleton wrote the play *Anything for a Quiet Life,* speaking through one of his characters: "E'en to seek out a quiet life, my lord; I do hear of a fine peaceable land . . . Gentlemen, fare you well, I am for the Bermudas."

Bermuda is still a fine, peaceable land. Indeed, in today's world, it prides itself on its social, civil, and natural order. Graeme Outerbridge's *Bermuda Abstracts* interprets this order with the island's most obvious symbol—its architecture. He isolates architectural essences with a clean, minimalist's eye, showing us a Bermuda we might otherwise fail to see.

Landt Dennis

Chimney Edge, Bermuda

Sunny Point, Southampton

Stamp House, Warwick

Atlas House, Hamilton

Mendham, Paget

Villa Cliff, Smith's Parish

Halcyon, Pembroke

The Jay's, Warwick

Near Ranger's, Southampton

Yellow House, Smith's

Harrison View, Southampton

Cap's Cottage, Pembroke

In the Pink, Smith's

Askew Cottage, Pembroke

Angel's Delight, Smith's

June Rose, Pembroke

Little Stirling, Devonshire

Hayden Trust, Sandy's

Garden Cottage, Paget

Bluebird, Tucker's Town

Rose Hill View, Southampton

Ely's Ridge, Somerset

Pillarville, Southampton

Pillarville, Southampton

Somewhere in Bermuda

Globe Press, Pembroke

Top Side, St. George's

Periwinkle, Paget

Foothills, Warwick

Somewhere in Bermuda

Park View, Southampton

Spice Berry, Warwick

Archway near Hamilton

Sunny-side, Southampton

Tucknoll, Southampton

Esso Station, Southampton

Watch House, Southampton

Somewhere in Bermuda

Richardson's House, Devonshire

Angel's Grotto, Smith's

Sugar Cane, Somerset

Vermilion Gable, Paget

Your Supermarket, St. George's

Your Supermarket, St. George's